Emerging Beyond The Scars

Your Daily Guide to Healing Trauma
and Finding Strength

Dr. Lisa M. Wineburg

Emerging Beyond the Scars
Your Daily Guide to Healing Trauma and Finding Strength
Dr. Lisa M. Wineburg

Published by Skinny Brown Dog Media
Atlanta, GA / Punta del Este, Uruguay

For Information, Contact:
Distributed by Skinny Brown Dog Media
SkinnyBrownDogMedia.com
Email: Info@SkinnyBrownDogMedia.com

Library of Congress Cataloging-in-Publication Data

ISBN (eBook)   978-1-965235-30-0
ISBN (trade paperback)   978-1-965235-89-8
ISBN (case laminate)   978-1-965235-31-7

CONTENTS

Dear Friend, ... ix
Why This Journal Matters. x
A Safe Place for Your Thoughts xi
Why We're Doing This Together xii

UNDERSTANDING
TRAUMA AND RESILIENCE

What is Trauma?. 3
What is Resilience? 5
Why Understanding Trauma and Resilience is Crucial for Your Growth . .6
How Trauma and Resilience Impact Different Aspects of Life 8

HOW TO USE THIS JOURNAL

Navigating the Journal 13
Understanding the Structure. 15
Creating a Daily Practice 17
Your Journey, Your Pace 19

PRE-SELF-ASSESSMENT

Section 1: Understanding of Trauma and Resilience 24
Section 2: Emotional and Physical Well-Being 28
Section 3: Setting Goals 31

WEEK 1
INTRODUCTION TO
TRAUMA AND RESILIENCE

Day 1: Introduction to Trauma and Resilience 37
Day 2: Understanding the Impact of Trauma 41
Day 3: Exploring Different Types of Trauma. 45
Day 4: Recognizing Trauma Symptoms 49
Day 5: Resilience in the Face of Trauma. 53
Day 6: Reframing Trauma as a Path to Growth 57
Day 7: Embracing Resilience and Setting Intentions. 61
Weekly Recap Week 1 Introduction to Trauma and Resilience. 65

WEEK 2
RECOGNIZING AND UNDERSTANDING
PERSONAL TRAUMA

Day 1: Identifying Personal Trauma 71
Day 2: Understanding the Emotional Impact of Trauma 75
Day 3: Exploring the Physical Manifestations of Trauma. 79
Day 4: Recognizing Trauma Triggers. 83
Day 5: Resilience in the Face of Trauma. 87
Day 6: Reframing Trauma as a Path to Growth 91
Day 7: Reflection and Growth 95
Weekly Recap Week 2 Recognizing and
    Understanding Personal Trauma. 99

WEEK 3
BUILDING EMOTIONAL RESILIENCE

Day 1: Emotional Awareness. 105
Day 2: Stress Management Techniques 109
Day 3: Cultivating a Positive Mindset 113
Day 4: Emotional Boundaries 117
Day 5: The Power of Gratitude 121
Day 6: Managing Emotional Overwhelm 125
Day 7: Reflection and Growth 129
Weekly Recap Week 3 Building Emotional Resilience 133

WEEK 4
CULTIVATING GROWTH
AND STRENGTH

Day 1: Recognizing Emotional Growth 139
Day 2: Building on Physical Strength 143
Day 3: Nurturing Personal Strengths 147
Day 4: Establishing Healthy Habits 151
Day 5: Integrating Emotional and Physical Growth. 155
Day 6: Overcoming Challenges in Growth. 159
Day 7: Reflection and Setting Intentions for Continued Growth. . . . 163
Weekly Recap Week 4 Cultivating Growth and Strength 167

POST-ASSESSMENT

Post-Assessment Structured Reflection 175

About the Author 181
Note About
  Beyond the Scars: Navigating Personal Growth After Trauma 183

DEDICATION

To you, the brave soul holding this journal—

This is for every step you've taken,
even when the path seemed impossible.
For every tear you've shed,
and every time you've picked yourself up again.
For the strength you've shown,
even in your most vulnerable moments.

You are not defined by your scars,
but by the incredible resilience that lies within you.

May this journal be a faithful companion on your journey,
A safe space for your thoughts, your fears, and your triumphs.
May it help you discover the wings you've always had,
And give you the courage to spread them and soar.

Remember, healing isn't a destination, but a journey.
And on this journey, you are never alone.

With deep respect and unwavering belief
in your ability to heal and thrive.

Dear Friend,

Welcome to The Foundations Journal. I know that opening up this journal is more than just turning a page—it's taking a courageous step on your journey of healing and growth. And for that, I want to thank you.

Why This Journal Matters

This journal was created with you in mind. As someone who has walked the path of trauma and resilience, I understand the complexities of healing. That's why I designed this journal to be a companion on your journey, a safe space where you can explore your feelings, reflect on your experiences, and discover your inner strength.

Drawing from the lessons in "Beyond the Scars," this journal provides daily prompts, exercises, and reflections that are all about helping you make sense of your story and build resilience. My hope is that as you write, you'll find new insights and tools that bring you closer to the healing and growth you deserve.

A Safe Place for Your Thoughts

I want you to know that this journal is yours—every word, every thought, and every reflection is for you alone. There's no right or wrong way to use it. Whether you're pouring your heart out on the page or jotting down a few words that come to mind, each entry is a meaningful step forward.

Healing is a deeply personal journey, and I encourage you to be gentle with yourself as you navigate through these pages. There may be moments of joy, moments of pain, and everything in between, and that's okay. All of it is part of the process, and every emotion you feel is valid.

Why We're Doing This Together

I wrote "Beyond the Scars" because I wanted to share the hope that even in our darkest moments, there is a path forward. This journal is a continuation of that message. It's a place where you can apply those lessons to your own life, day by day, with the support and encouragement you need.

I'm with you every step of the way, cheering you on as you explore your thoughts and feelings. Together, we'll uncover the resilience that lies within you, and you'll begin to see that no matter what you've been through, you have the strength to heal and grow.

Thank you for trusting me to be a part of your journey. I'm honored to walk alongside you, and I can't wait to see where this journal takes you.

With love and encouragement,

Dr. W.

Understanding Trauma and Resilience

As we begin this journey together, I want to take some time to explore two crucial concepts that will guide much of our work in this journal: trauma and resilience. These aren't just abstract ideas—they're experiences that shape the way we live, love, and grow. By understanding them more deeply, we can begin to navigate the complexities of our past and move toward a future filled with healing and hope.

What is Trauma?

Trauma is something that most of us have experienced in some form or another. It might be a sudden, life-altering event like an accident, a loss, or a devastating diagnosis. Or it might be something that happened gradually, like the slow erosion of your self-worth in a toxic relationship, or the ongoing stress of living in an unsafe environment. In Beyond the Scars, I explore how trauma is not just about what happens to us, but about how those events affect us, often in ways we might not fully understand at first.

Trauma can leave us feeling lost, isolated, and overwhelmed. It can affect us emotionally, causing feelings of fear, anxiety, or deep sadness that seem impossible to shake. It can manifest physically, leading to chronic pain, fatigue, or other health issues. Mentally, trauma can change the way we think and process information, leading to difficulties with concentration, memory, or decision-making. Spiritually, trauma can shake our faith or our sense of purpose, leaving us questioning our place in the world.

In Beyond the Scars, I discuss how trauma is like a wound—one that isn't always visible to the outside world, but that continues to ache long after the initial event has passed. This wound can influence how we see ourselves, how we relate to others, and how we move through the world. It can make us feel as though we're carrying an invisible burden, one that weighs us down in ways that are hard to explain to others.

But here's an important truth: while trauma can have a profound impact on our lives, it does not define us. You are not just what has happened to you. You are also your response to what has happened, and that's where the concept of resilience comes in.

What is Resilience?

Resilience is a word that gets used a lot these days, but it's more than just a buzzword—it's a powerful tool that can help us navigate the challenges that life throws our way. In Beyond the Scars, I define resilience as the ability to adapt to adversity, to recover from setbacks, and to continue growing, even in the face of overwhelming odds. Resilience is not about pretending that everything is fine, or about ignoring the pain of our experiences. Instead, it's about acknowledging the hurt, while also finding the strength to move forward.

One of the most important lessons in Beyond the Scars is that resilience isn't something you either have or don't have. It's a skill—a set of behaviors, thoughts, and actions that you can learn and strengthen over time. Every time you face a challenge and choose to keep going, you're building resilience. Every time you ask for help, take a moment to care for yourself, or find a way to look at a situation differently, you're practicing resilience.

In the book, I share stories of individuals who have faced unimaginable challenges—loss, abuse, illness—and yet have found ways to not only survive but to thrive. These stories are powerful reminders that resilience is within all of us, waiting to be tapped into. It's about finding that inner strength that says, "I may be knocked down, but I'm not out."

Why Understanding Trauma and Resilience is Crucial for Your Growth

So why does all of this matter? Why are we focusing so much on trauma and resilience in this journal? Because understanding these two concepts is key to unlocking your potential for growth and healing.

When we start to understand trauma, we begin to see the patterns in our lives—the ways that past hurts have influenced our thoughts, behaviors, and emotions. This awareness is the first step toward healing because it allows us to address the root causes of our pain rather than just treating the symptoms. In Beyond the Scars, I emphasize that recognizing the impact of trauma is not about dwelling on the past, but about empowering ourselves to move forward with greater clarity and strength.

Resilience, on the other hand, is about what comes next. It's about how we take that understanding of trauma and use it to build a life that is not just about survival, but about thriving. Resilience allows us to face new challenges with confidence, knowing that we have the tools and the strength to overcome them. It helps us to maintain our sense of self-worth and purpose, even when life gets tough.

Throughout this journal, you'll find prompts, exercises, and reflections that are designed to help you explore these concepts in a way that is personal and meaningful to you. I've drawn on the teachings from Beyond the Scars to create a space where you can delve into your experiences, understand how they've shaped you, and begin the process of transforming your pain into power.

As you work through this journal, I want you to remember that this is your journey. There is no right or wrong way to do this. Some days you might feel like you're making great progress, and other days you might feel like you're struggling to move forward at all. Both of these experiences are valid, and both are part of the process of healing.

In Beyond the Scars, I often talk about the idea of growth not being a straight line, but a series of peaks and valleys. There will be days when you feel strong and resilient, and there will be days when you feel overwhelmed and vulnerable. Both are okay. What matters is that you keep moving forward, even if it's just one small step at a time.

How Trauma and Resilience Impact Different Aspects of Life

Trauma and resilience don't just affect one part of us—they touch every aspect of our lives. Here's a quick overview of how these concepts can play out across different areas:

- Emotionally: Trauma can leave us feeling disconnected from our emotions, or it can make us feel like we're drowning in them. Resilience helps us to reconnect with our feelings in a healthy way, to process them, and to find a sense of balance.
- Physically: Trauma often manifests in our bodies, whether through chronic pain, fatigue, or other health issues. Resilience involves caring for our bodies, recognizing when we need rest or support, and finding ways to build physical strength and well-being.
- Mentally: Trauma can disrupt our thinking, making it hard to concentrate, make decisions, or even remember things. Resilience helps us to regain our mental clarity, to focus on the present, and to plan for the future.
- Spiritually: Trauma can shake our faith or our sense of purpose, leaving us questioning why things have happened the way they have. Resilience helps us to rebuild our spiritual foundation, to find meaning in our experiences, and to connect with something larger than ourselves.

Each of these areas is interconnected. As you begin to heal emotionally, you might find that your physical health improves. As you build mental resilience, your spiritual life might become richer and more fulfilling. The journey you're on is holistic—it's about nurturing every part of who you are.

Moving Forward Together

As you dive into this journal, I want you to keep the concepts of trauma and resilience in mind. Use them as lenses through which to view your experiences, and as tools to help you navigate the challenges ahead. Remember, understanding your trauma is not about defining yourself by it—it's about freeing yourself from its grip. And building resilience is not about never falling down—it's about knowing that you have the strength to get back up, no matter how many times life knocks you over.

In Beyond the Scars, I wrote that healing is not just about what we do, but about how we think and how we view ourselves. This journal is an opportunity for you to start thinking of yourself not just as a survivor, but as a person with incredible strength and potential. It's a chance to start seeing your scars not as signs of weakness, but as badges of honor—proof of your resilience and your ability to overcome.

Thank you, again, for allowing me to be a part of your journey. I'm here with you every step of the way, and I believe in your ability to heal, to grow, and to thrive. Let's move forward together, with hope, with courage, and with the understanding that you are so much more than your scars.

How to Use This Journal

I'm so glad you're here, ready to begin your journey with The Foundations Journal. This journal is designed to be a supportive companion as you navigate your path toward healing and resilience. To help you get the most out of it, I'd like to walk you through how to use this journal, what to expect from its structure, and how you can create a daily practice that feels meaningful and nourishing.

Navigating the Journal

This journal is meant to be your safe space—a place where you can express yourself freely and explore your thoughts and feelings without judgment. Here's how you can navigate through it:

- Daily Prompts: Each day, you'll find a specific prompt designed to guide your reflection. These prompts are crafted to help you explore your experiences with trauma, recognize your strengths, and build resilience. You might find that some prompts resonate deeply with you, while others challenge you to think in new ways. That's okay—there's no right or wrong way to engage with these prompts. Simply approach each one with an open heart and a willingness to explore.
- Weekly Themes: At the beginning of each week, you'll encounter a new theme that sets the tone for the days ahead. These themes are aligned with the teachings in Beyond the Scars and are meant to help you focus on different aspects of your healing journey. For example, one week might be dedicated to understanding trauma, while another focuses on building emotional resilience. These themes provide a framework for your reflections, helping you to dive deeper into specific areas of your life.
- Weekly Reflections: At the end of each week, you'll have a chance to look back and reflect on what you've learned.

These reflections are an opportunity to process your experiences, celebrate your progress, and identify areas where you'd like to continue growing. Take this time to be gentle with yourself—acknowledge the challenges you've faced, but also honor the strength you've shown.

- Assessments: Both at the beginning and end of the journal, you'll find self-assessments that are designed to help you gauge your progress. The initial assessment will give you a sense of where you're starting from, while the final assessment will allow you to reflect on how far you've come. These assessments include both rating scales and open-ended questions, giving you a comprehensive picture of your emotional, physical, mental, and spiritual well-being.

Understanding the Structure

To make it easier for you to move through the journal, I've structured it in a way that builds upon itself each day and week. Here's a quick overview of what to expect:

- Daily Prompts: Each day's prompt is designed to guide you through a specific aspect of trauma and resilience. These prompts encourage introspection, helping you to uncover patterns, identify strengths, and recognize areas where you might want to focus your healing efforts. The prompts are varied, so some days you might be reflecting on a specific memory, while other days you might be exploring your emotions or planning ways to take care of yourself.
- Weekly Themes: The weekly themes are designed to provide a deeper focus on particular aspects of your journey. For instance, Week 1 might focus on understanding the basics of trauma and resilience, while Week 2 dives into recognizing and processing personal trauma. As you move through the journal, each week builds upon the last, helping you to gradually deepen your understanding and strengthen your resilience.
- Guided Visualizations and Mindfulness Activities: Interwoven with the prompts are guided visualizations and mindfulness exercises. These practices are designed to help you connect with your inner self, calm your mind, and cultivate a sense of peace. These activities are especially

helpful when you're feeling overwhelmed or need a moment of grounding.

- Progress Tracking: To help you see your growth, there are spaces for tracking your emotional and physical responses each week. This might include noting your mood, energy levels, or any significant changes in your well-being. By keeping track of these responses, you can begin to identify patterns and recognize how your efforts are paying off.

Creating a Daily Practice

One of the most important things you can do for yourself as you work through this journal is to create a daily practice that feels supportive and sustainable. Here are a few suggestions to help you get started:

- Set Aside Time: Healing and reflection take time, so I encourage you to set aside a specific time each day to engage with this journal. It might be first thing in the morning, before the busyness of the day takes over, or it could be in the evening, when you have some quiet time to yourself. Even just 10 to 15 minutes a day can make a big difference.
- Create a Comfortable Space: Find a spot where you feel comfortable and safe—whether it's a cozy chair, your bed, or a quiet corner of your home. This is your space to relax and reflect, so make it as inviting as possible. Maybe light a candle, play some soft music, or have a warm cup of tea nearby.
- Be Consistent but Flexible: While consistency is important, it's also okay to be flexible with yourself. There might be days when you don't feel up to writing, and that's okay. If you miss a day, don't worry—just come back when you're ready. This journal is here to support you, not to add pressure.

- Start with Gratitude: A great way to begin each journaling session is by taking a moment to think about something you're grateful for. Gratitude helps to shift our focus from what's lacking to what's abundant in our lives, and it can be a powerful tool in your healing journey.
- Reflect and Review: At the end of each week, take some time to review what you've written. Reflect on the insights you've gained, the challenges you've faced, and the progress you've made. This reflection time is a chance to celebrate your growth and set intentions for the week ahead.

Your Journey, Your Pace

Remember, this journal is a tool for your healing, and you have the freedom to use it in whatever way feels right for you. There's no rush—take your time and move at a pace that feels comfortable. Some days, you might find that you want to spend more time reflecting, while other days, a quick check-in might be all you need. Both are perfectly okay.

As you work through the prompts and exercises, keep in mind that this is your journey. Be kind to yourself, and allow yourself to experience whatever comes up, whether it's joy, pain, or anything in between. Healing is not a linear process, but with each day that you engage with this journal, you're taking a step forward on your path to resilience and growth.

Pre-Self-Assessment

As you begin your journey with The Foundations Journal, it's important to take some time to reflect on where you are right now. This self-assessment is designed to help you gain a clearer understanding of your current state—emotionally, physically, and mentally—before diving into the work ahead. By honestly evaluating your starting point, you'll be better equipped to set meaningful goals and track your progress throughout the next 30 days.

The self-assessment is divided into three sections, each serving a distinct purpose

Section 1 Understanding of Trauma and Resilience

This section is intended to help you explore your current understanding of trauma and resilience. By reflecting on how these concepts have played a role in your life so far, you'll gain insights into how past experiences have shaped you and identify the strengths you already possess. This foundational knowledge will guide you as you work through the journal, helping you build on what you know and address any areas where you wish to deepen your understanding.

Section 2 Emotional and Physical Well-Being

Your emotional and physical well-being are deeply interconnected and play a crucial role in your ability to heal and grow. In this section, you'll assess your current state of well-being through a series of rating scales and reflective questions. This assessment will help you identify areas that may need more attention and care, providing a baseline for the progress you'll make over the next 30 days.

Section 3 Setting Goals

Setting clear, intentional goals is a key part of any journey toward personal growth. In this section, you'll define what you hope to achieve over the next 30 days. Whether it's building resilience, gaining a better understanding of your trauma, or improving your overall well-being, setting goals will give you a sense of direction and purpose. This will be your roadmap, guiding you through the challenges and triumphs ahead.

How to Use This Self-Assessment

Take your time as you work through each section of the self-assessment. There's no need to rush—this is about understanding where you are so that you can move forward with clarity and intention. Be honest with yourself as you answer the questions and reflect on your responses. Remember, this is your journey, and every step you take—no matter how small—brings you closer to healing and growth.

Once you've completed the self-assessment, keep it in mind as you work through the journal. You'll find that these initial reflections will provide valuable insights as you set goals, track your progress, and celebrate your achievements along the way.

Section 1
Understanding of Trauma and Resilience

Personal Self-Assessment Quiz Understanding Trauma and Resilience

Take a few moments to answer the following questions. This quiz is designed to help you explore your current understanding of trauma and resilience, as well as to reflect on your past experiences and coping mechanisms. There's no right or wrong answer—this is all about where you are right now.

1. How would you define trauma?
   - ☐ A specific, life-changing event
   - ☐ A series of challenging experiences over time
   - ☐ Something that deeply impacts my emotions, thoughts, and behavior
   - ☐ Other: _____

Reflect: In your own words, write down what trauma means to you.
Your Response: _____

2. How do you understand the concept of resilience?
    ☐ The ability to bounce back after difficulties
    ☐ A skill that can be learned and strengthened
    ☐ A mindset that helps me cope with challenges
    ☐ Other: _____

    Reflect: Describe how you see resilience playing a role in your life.
    Your Response: _____

3. What role do you believe trauma has played in your life so far?
    ☐ It has significantly shaped my relationships
    ☐ It has influenced how I see myself
    ☐ It has impacted my physical and emotional well-being
    ☐ Other: _____

    Reflect: Think about how trauma has affected various aspects
    of your life.
    Your Response: _____

4. In what ways do you feel resilient?
    ☐ I've overcome significant challenges in my life
    ☐ I've found ways to keep going, even when it's tough
    ☐ I can manage my emotions during difficult times
    ☐ Other: _____

    Reflect: Consider the strengths you've shown in challenging
    situations.
    Your Response: _____

5. How do you currently cope with stress or difficult emotions?
    ☐ I talk to friends or family for support
    ☐ I engage in activities like exercise, meditation, or hobbies
    ☐ I try to avoid thinking about what's bothering me
    ☐ Other: _____

Reflect: Assess your current coping mechanisms—are they helpful or could they be improved?
Your Response: _____

Reflection on Past Experiences

6. Can you recall a specific experience of trauma that has had a significant impact on you?

    Reflect: Write down a memory or period in your life that stands out as particularly challenging.
    Your Response: _____

7. How have you typically responded to trauma in the past?
    ☐ With strong emotions (anger, sadness, fear)
    ☐ By withdrawing or isolating myself
    ☐ By seeking help or support
    ☐ Other: _____

    Reflect: Describe your usual reactions to trauma.
    Your Response: _____

8. What coping mechanisms did you develop in response to trauma?
    ☐ Positive strategies (seeking support, self-care)
    ☐ Avoidance or self-isolation
    ☐ Turning to unhealthy habits (e.g., overeating, substance use)
    ☐ Other: _____

    Reflect: Identify the strategies you've used to cope with trauma.
    Your Response: _____

9. Have your coping mechanisms evolved over time?
    ☐ Yes, I've developed healthier ways to cope
    ☐ No, I rely on the same strategies as before
    ☐ I'm not sure
    ☐ Other: _____

    Reflect: Think about how your coping strategies have changed over the years.
    Your Response: _____

10. What are the areas where you feel your coping strategies could improve?

    Reflect: Consider where you'd like to see change in how you handle stress or trauma.
    Your Response: _____

Section 2
Emotional and Physical Well-Being

Before we go further, it's important to take a closer look at your current state of emotional and physical well-being. This assessment will help you reflect on how you're feeling right now, both emotionally and physically, so you can better understand your needs as you move through this journal. Remember, this is about gaining insight, not judgment—so approach this section with honesty and self-compassion.

Rating Scales to Assess Your Current Well-Being

1. How would you rate your current level of stress?
   - On a scale of 1 to 10, with 1 being very low stress and 10 being extremely high stress, where do you find yourself today?
   - Your Rating: _____

2. How well do you feel you are managing your emotions?
   - Consider how well you handle your emotions, especially in challenging situations. Rate yourself on a scale of 1 to 10, with 1 being very poorly and 10 being exceptionally well.
   - Your Rating: _____

3. How would you describe the quality of your sleep?
    *   Reflect on your recent sleep patterns. On a scale of 1 to 10, with 1 being very poor sleep and 10 being excellent sleep, how well are you resting?
    *   Your Rating: _____

4. How would you rate your energy levels throughout the day?
    *   Think about how much energy you have on a typical day. On a scale of 1 to 10, with 1 being very low energy and 10 being very high energy, how would you rate yourself?
    *   Your Rating: _____

5. Overall, how would you rate your well-being right now?
    *   Take a moment to reflect on your overall well-being. On a scale of 1 to 10, with 1 being poor and 10 being excellent, where do you currently stand?
    *   Your Rating: _____

Questions to Explore Your Emotional State

1. How are you feeling emotionally at this moment?
    *   Are you feeling anxious, depressed, hopeful, or something else? Write down the emotions that come up for you as you reflect on your current state.

2. What factors are influencing your emotional state right now?
    *   Consider what might be contributing to your current feelings. Is it a particular event, ongoing stress, or something else? Reflect on the underlying causes of your emotional state.

3. How do your emotions affect your daily life?
   - Think about how your emotions impact your day-to-day activities, relationships, and decisions. Are there specific emotions that have a stronger influence on you?

4. What steps do you take to manage feelings of anxiety or depression?
   - Reflect on the strategies you use to cope with difficult emotions. Are they effective, or do you feel there's room for improvement?

5. What gives you hope or lifts your spirits?
   - Consider the sources of hope or joy in your life. What helps you stay positive, even during challenging times?

This section is intended to help you get a clearer picture of where you stand emotionally and physically as you begin this journal. Understanding these aspects of yourself can guide you in setting meaningful intentions and goals for the next 30 days, allowing you to focus on the areas that need the most attention and care.

Section 3
Setting Goals

Personal Goal-Setting Quiz: Setting Intentions for Your Journey

As you prepare to embark on this 30-day journey, it's important to set clear and meaningful goals that will guide your progress. This quiz is designed to help you identify what you hope to achieve and the areas where you wish to grow. Reflect on each question honestly—this is your opportunity to focus on what truly matters to you.

1. What do you hope to achieve over the next 30 days?
   - ☐ Develop healthier coping mechanisms
   - ☐ Gain a deeper understanding of my trauma
   - ☐ Build resilience in specific areas of my life
   - ☐ Improve my overall well-being
   - ☐ Other: _____

   Reflect: Describe the specific changes or improvements you'd like to see by the end of this journal.
   Your Response: _____

2. In which areas of your life do you feel you need the most growth?
   - ☐ Emotional well-being
   - ☐ Physical health

□ Mental clarity and focus
□ Spiritual connection
□ Other: _____

Reflect: Reflect on the aspects of your life where you believe growth is most needed.
Your Response: _____

3. How would you like to build resilience during this journey?
   □ By developing better stress management techniques
   □ By learning to navigate challenges with more confidence
   □ By cultivating a more positive mindset
   □ Other: _____

Reflect: Consider how you want to strengthen your resilience over the next 30 days.
Your Response: _____

4. What do you want to learn or understand better about your trauma?
   □ The root causes of my trauma
   □ How my trauma affects my current behavior
   □ Strategies for healing and recovery
   □ Other: _____

Reflect: Identify the specific aspects of your trauma that you want to explore and understand more deeply.
Your Response: _____

5. What positive changes do you hope to see in yourself by the end of this journal?
   □ Increased self-awareness
   □ Greater emotional stability

☐ Improved relationships
☐ Enhanced physical and mental health
☐ Other: _____

Reflect: Think about the personal growth you want to achieve and the positive changes you're hoping to see.
Your Response: _____

     This goal-setting quiz is designed to help you clarify your intentions and focus on what you want to achieve during this journey. By reflecting on these questions, you'll be able to set meaningful goals that align with your personal needs and desires, guiding you through the next 30 days with purpose and direction.

Week 1
Introduction to Trauma and Resilience

Day 1
Introduction to Trauma and Resilience

"The wound is the place where the Light enters you."
— Rumi

Focus

Today, we begin our journey by exploring what trauma is and how it impacts our lives. Trauma can come in many forms—whether it's a sudden event, ongoing stress, or something more complex. Understanding the nature of trauma is the first step toward healing.

Daily Prompt

Take a moment to think about the word "trauma." What does it mean to you? Reflect on any experiences in your life that you would identify as traumatic. How have these experiences affected you emotionally, mentally, and physically?

Exercise

- Reflective Writing: Spend 10-15 minutes writing about a specific traumatic experience that has had a significant impact on you. Focus on how it made you feel at the time and how it continues to influence your life today.
- Identifying Resilience: Think about how you responded to this trauma. What personal strengths did you draw upon to get through it? Write down at least one instance where you showed resilience.

_____

_____

_____

_____

_____

Visualization and Mindfulness

Grounding Exercise: Sit comfortably and close your eyes. Take a few deep breaths, focusing on the sensation of the breath moving in and out of your body. Visualize yourself as a strong, rooted tree, with deep roots extending into the earth. Feel the stability and strength that comes from being grounded. This exercise helps you stay present and connected to the here and now.

Tools for Tracking Emotional and Physical Progress

At the end of each day, take a few minutes to reflect on your emotional and physical state. Use the following simple scales to track your progress:

1. Emotional State:
   On a scale of 1 to 10, how would you rate your emotional state today? (1 = Very low, 10 = Very high)
   Your Rating: _____

2. Physical Energy:
   On a scale of 1 to 10, how would you rate your energy levels today? (1 = Very low, 10 = Very high)
   Your Rating: _____

3. Overall Well-Being:
   On a scale of 1 to 10, how would you rate your overall well-being today? (1 = Poor, 10 = Excellent)
   Your Rating: _____

Reflection

Write one or two sentences reflecting on why you gave the ratings above. Consider how the day's activities, emotions, or physical state influenced these ratings.

Example

"Today, I felt a lot of emotional weight as I reflected on my trauma, so I rated my emotional state at a 4. However, the grounding exercise helped me feel more centered, so my physical energy felt like a 7. Overall, I would rate my well-being at a 6 because, despite the heaviness, I feel like I'm making progress."

Great! Here are the prompts, exercises, and tools for tracking emotional and physical progress for Days 2-7, each with an inspirational quote that aligns with the day's focus.

Day 2
Understanding the Impact of Trauma

*"You may not control all the events that happen to you,
but you can decide not to be reduced by them."*
— Maya Angelou

Focus

Today, we'll explore the wide-reaching effects that
trauma can have on different aspects of your life, including your
relationships, work, and sense of self.

Daily Prompt

Reflect on how trauma has impacted your life in various
ways. Consider your relationships, work, and self-perception. How
has trauma influenced your decisions, behaviors, and emotions?

Exercise

- Reflective Writing: Write about a specific way trauma has
  affected your life, focusing on one area (e.g., relationships

or work). How has it changed your behavior, thoughts, or feelings in that area?

- Identifying Impact: List three ways that trauma has influenced your life, and then note one strength you've developed in response to each of these challenges.

_____

_____

_____

_____

_____

Visualization and Mindfulness

Breathing Exercise: Practice deep breathing to calm your mind and body. Inhale slowly for a count of 4, hold for 4, and exhale for 6. Repeat this cycle for 5 minutes, focusing on the sensation of your breath.

Tools for Tracking Emotional and Physical Progress

1. Emotional State:
   Your Rating: _____

2. Physical Energy:
   Your Rating: _____

3. Overall Well-Being:
   Your Rating: _____

Reflection

Write one or two sentences reflecting on your emotional and physical ratings today.

Day 3
Exploring Different Types of Trauma

*"Out of suffering have emerged the strongest souls;
the most massive characters are seared with scars."*
– Kahlil Gibran

Focus

Today, we'll delve into the different types of traumas—acute, chronic, and complex—and how each one uniquely affects individuals.

Daily Prompt

Consider which type(s) of trauma you have experienced—acute (a single event), chronic (repeated or prolonged trauma), or complex (multiple traumatic events). How have these experiences shaped your life?

Exercise

- Reflective Writing: Identify a type of trauma that resonates with your experience. Write about how it has influenced your emotional and mental well-being.

- Exploring Impact: Choose one type of trauma and list the ways it has impacted your daily life. Include both challenges and any coping strategies you've developed.

_____

_____

_____

_____

_____

Visualization and Mindfulness

Mindful Observation: Spend 5 minutes observing your surroundings in silence. Focus on the details—colors, textures, sounds—without judgment. This practice helps in staying grounded in the present moment.

Tools for Tracking Emotional and Physical Progress

1. Emotional State:
   Your Rating: _____

2. Physical Energy:
   Your Rating: _____

3. Overall Well-Being:
   Your Rating: _____

Reflection

Write one or two sentences reflecting on your emotional and physical ratings today.

Day 4
Recognizing Trauma Symptoms

"Although the world is full of suffering,
it is also full of the overcoming of it."
— Helen Keller

Focus

Today, we'll identify common symptoms of trauma—both emotional and physical—and how they manifest in your daily life.

Daily Prompt

Reflect on the symptoms of trauma you've experienced. These might include anxiety, flashbacks, avoidance, or physical symptoms like headaches or fatigue. How do these symptoms affect your life?

Exercise

- Reflective Writing: Write about a symptom of trauma that you experience regularly. How does it impact your daily routine or interactions with others?

- Symptom Recognition: Make a list of the trauma symptoms you've noticed in yourself. For each one, note how it affects you and what, if anything, you've done to manage it.

_____

_____

_____

_____

_____

Visualization and Mindfulness

Body Scan Meditation: Sit or lie down comfortably. Close your eyes and slowly scan your body from head to toe, noticing any tension or discomfort. Breathe into these areas, imagining the tension melting away with each exhale.

Tools for Tracking Emotional and Physical Progress

1. Emotional State:
   Your Rating: _____

2. Physical Energy:
   Your Rating: _____

3. Overall Well-Being:
   Your Rating: _____

Reflection

Write one or two sentences reflecting on your emotional and physical ratings today.

Day 5
Resilience in the Face of Trauma

---

*"Do not judge me by my success, judge me by how
many times I fell down and got back up again."*
— Nelson Mandela

Focus

Today, we'll focus on the concept of resilience and how you've demonstrated resilience in the face of trauma. Resilience isn't just about surviving; it's about finding ways to thrive despite challenges.

Daily Prompt

Reflect on a time when you demonstrated resilience. What did you do to cope with the challenge, and what strengths did you discover in yourself?

Exercise

- Reflective Writing: Write about a specific instance where you bounced back from a difficult situation. What personal qualities helped you persevere?

- Resilience Inventory: List three personal strengths that have helped you navigate trauma. For each strength, write about a time when it served you well.

_____

_____

_____

_____

_____

Visualization and Mindfulness

Visualization of Strength: Close your eyes and visualize yourself overcoming a challenge. Imagine the strength and resilience you used in that moment and let that feeling fill your body with confidence.

Tools for Tracking Emotional and Physical Progress

1. Emotional State:
   Your Rating: _____

2. Physical Energy:
   Your Rating: _____

3. Overall Well-Being:
   Your Rating: _____

Reflection

Write one or two sentences reflecting on your emotional and physical ratings today.

_____

_____

_____

_____

_____

_____

_____

_____

_____

_____

_____

_____

_____

_____

_____

Day 6
Reframing Trauma as a Path to Growth

"The human capacity for burden is like bamboo—far more flexible than you'd ever believe at first glance."
— Jodi Picoult

Focus

Today, we'll explore the idea of post-traumatic growth—the concept that, through facing and overcoming trauma, we can develop new strengths, perspectives, and a deeper appreciation for life.

Daily Prompt

Consider how your trauma has changed you—not just in terms of the pain, but in terms of the growth it has prompted. What positive changes have emerged from your challenges?

Exercise

- Reflective Writing: Write about a way in which you've grown as a result of your trauma. What new strengths, insights, or perspectives have you gained?

- Growth Visualization: Imagine your life as a garden. Reflect on how the "seeds" of your trauma have grown into something new and strong. Write about what your garden looks like now, and what you hope it will become.

_____

_____

_____

_____

_____

Visualization and Mindfulness

Visualization of Growth: Close your eyes and visualize a seed growing into a strong tree. As the tree grows, imagine your own personal growth and strength expanding, despite the storms it has weathered.

Tools for Tracking Emotional and Physical Progress

1. Emotional State:
   Your Rating: _____

2. Physical Energy:
   Your Rating: _____

3. Overall Well-Being:
   Your Rating: _____

Reflection

Write one or two sentences reflecting on your emotional and physical ratings today.

Day 7
Embracing Resilience
and Setting Intentions

"Life doesn't get easier or more forgiving;
we get stronger and more resilient."
— Steve Maraboli

Focus

Today marks the end of our first week. We'll reflect on the lessons learned about trauma and resilience and set intentions for the coming weeks.

Daily Prompt

Reflect on what you've learned about trauma and resilience this week. How has your understanding evolved, and what intentions do you want to set moving forward?

Exercise

- Reflective Writing: Summarize the key insights you've gained this week. What stood out to you the most? What areas do you want to focus on in the coming weeks?
- Setting Intentions: Write down three intentions for the next week. These might be areas of focus, attitudes you want to cultivate, or practices you want to continue.

_____

_____

_____

_____

_____

Visualization and Mindfulness

Mindful Breathing: Spend a few minutes in mindful breathing, focusing on the breath as it enters and leaves your body. With each exhale, let go of any tension or stress from the past week. With each inhale, invite in calm and focus for the week ahead.

Tools for Tracking Emotional and Physical Progress

1. Emotional State:
   Your Rating: _____

2. Physical Energy:
   Your Rating: _____

3. Overall Well-Being:
   Your Rating: _____

Reflection

Write one or two sentences reflecting on your emotional and physical ratings today.

Weekly Recap
Week 1
Introduction to Trauma and Resilience

Reflecting on Your Journey

Congratulations on completing your first week! This week, you've taken important steps in understanding trauma and building resilience. You've explored the impact of trauma on your life, recognized symptoms, and identified the strengths that have helped you navigate through challenging times.

Key Insights

1. Understanding Trauma:
   You've reflected on what trauma means to you and how it has influenced various aspects of your life. Recognizing these impacts is crucial for your healing journey.

2. Identifying Resilience:
   You've begun to uncover the strengths you've developed in response to trauma. These strengths are the foundation of your resilience.

3. Exploring Growth:
   You've considered how trauma, while painful, has also prompted personal growth. This understanding opens the door to post-traumatic growth, where you can transform your experiences into sources of strength and wisdom.

Tracking Your Progress

Now, let's take a moment to look back at your emotional and physical well-being over the past week. Review your daily ratings for emotional state, physical energy, and overall well-being. Consider the following prompt as you reflect on the patterns you've noticed:

Progress Reflection Prompt

What patterns have you observed in your emotional and physical well-being this week?

- Were there specific days when you felt particularly strong or vulnerable?
- What factors contributed to these fluctuations?
- How did the exercises and mindfulness practices influence your well-being?

Your Reflection

_____

_____

_____

_____

_____

_____

Looking Ahead

As you prepare for the next week, think about the areas where you'd like to focus your energy. What lessons from this week will you carry forward? What intentions do you want to set for the upcoming days?

Setting Intentions

- Intention 1: _____
- Intention 2: _____
- Intention 3: _____

Remember, this journey is about progress, not perfection. Celebrate the steps you've taken this week and look forward to the growth that lies ahead. You're doing incredible work—keep moving forward with strength and resilience.

Week 2
Recognizing and Understanding Personal Trauma

Day 1
Identifying Personal Trauma

---

*"Healing doesn't mean the damage never existed.
It means the damage no longer controls our lives."*
— Unknown

Focus

Today, we begin to deepen our understanding of trauma by identifying the specific events or experiences in your life that you consider traumatic. Recognizing these experiences is a crucial first step toward healing.

Daily Prompt

Reflect on the specific events or experiences in your life that you would identify as traumatic. How do these events continue to affect you today, emotionally, mentally, and physically?

Exercise

- Reflective Writing: Write about a personal trauma that has had a significant impact on your life. Focus on how it made you feel at the time and how it continues to influence your thoughts, behaviors, and emotions today.

- Exploring Impact: Identify three ways that this trauma has influenced your life. Then, note one strength you've developed in response to each of these challenges.

_____

_____

_____

_____

_____

Visualization and Mindfulness

- Breathing Exercise: Practice deep breathing to calm your mind and body. Inhale slowly for a count of 4, hold for 4, and exhale for 6. Repeat this cycle for 5 minutes, focusing on the sensation of your breath.

Tools for Tracking Emotional and Physical Progress

1. Emotional State:
   On a scale of 1 to 10, how would you rate your emotional state today? (1 = Very low, 10 = Very high)
   Your Rating: _____

2. Physical Energy:
   On a scale of 1 to 10, how would you rate your energy levels today? (1 = Very low, 10 = Very high)
   Your Rating: _____

3. Overall Well-Being:
   On a scale of 1 to 10, how would you rate your overall
   well-being today? (1 = Poor, 10 = Excellent)
   Your Rating: _____

Reflection

Write one or two sentences reflecting on why you gave
the ratings above. Consider how the day's activities, emotions, or
physical state influenced these ratings.

Example Reflection

"Today, I felt a mix of emotions as I reflected on my trauma.
My emotional state felt heavy, so I rated it at a 5. However, the
deep breathing exercise helped calm my mind, so my physical
energy felt like a 6. Overall, I would rate my well-being at a 5
because, although the memories were difficult, acknowledging
them felt like a step toward healing."

Day 2
Understanding the Emotional Impact of Trauma

"You may not control all the events that happen to you,
but you can decide not to be reduced by them."
— Maya Angelou

Focus

Today, we'll explore the wide-reaching effects that trauma can have on your emotions. Understanding how trauma impacts your emotional landscape is a crucial step in the healing process.

Daily Prompt

Reflect on how trauma has affected your emotions over time. Consider both the immediate emotional responses to trauma and the lingering effects. How have these emotional impacts influenced your decisions, behaviors, and relationships?

Exercise

- Reflective Writing: Write about a specific way trauma has affected your emotional well-being. Focus on one area, such as how it has influenced your relationships or your ability to cope with stress.
- Identifying Emotional Impact: List three emotional responses that have been shaped by your trauma. For each, note how these emotions have impacted your daily life and what strengths you have developed to manage them.

_____

_____

_____

_____

_____

Visualization and Mindfulness

- Grounding Exercise: Take a few moments to center yourself in the present. Sit comfortably, close your eyes, and take deep breaths. As you inhale, imagine drawing in calm energy; as you exhale, let go of any tension or anxiety. Repeat this for 5 minutes, focusing on staying grounded and connected to the present moment.

Tools for Tracking Emotional and Physical Progress

1. Emotional State:
   On a scale of 1 to 10, how would you rate your emotional state today? (1 = Very low, 10 = Very high)
   Your Rating: _____

2. Physical Energy:
   On a scale of 1 to 10, how would you rate your energy levels today? (1 = Very low, 10 = Very high)
   Your Rating: _____

3. Overall Well-Being:
   On a scale of 1 to 10, how would you rate your overall well-being today? (1 = Poor, 10 = Excellent)
   Your Rating: _____

Reflection

Write one or two sentences reflecting on why you gave the ratings above. Consider how the day's activities, emotions, or physical state influenced these ratings.

Example Reflection

"Today, reflecting on the emotional impact of trauma brought up some sadness, so I rated my emotional state at a 4. The grounding exercise helped me feel more present, which boosted my energy to a 6. Overall, I would rate my well-being at a 5 because I felt both the weight of past emotions and the relief of staying grounded."

_____

_____

_____

_____

_____

_____

_____

_____

_____

_____

_____

_____

_____

Day 3
Exploring the Physical Manifestations of Trauma

"Your body keeps the score."
— Bessel van der Kolk

Focus

Today, we'll explore how trauma affects the body. Trauma can manifest physically in various ways, such as chronic pain, fatigue, or other health issues. Understanding these physical responses is essential for comprehensive healing.

Daily Prompt

Reflect on how trauma has impacted your body. Do you experience physical symptoms like headaches, muscle tension, or fatigue that you believe are related to your trauma? How do these physical symptoms affect your daily life?

Exercise

- Reflective Writing: Write about any physical symptoms or discomforts that you believe are connected to your trauma. How do these symptoms manifest, and how have they influenced your overall well-being?
- Exploring Physical Impact: Identify three physical symptoms that you associate with your trauma. For each, note how it affects your daily activities and what strategies you use to manage it.

_____

_____

_____

_____

_____

Visualization and Mindfulness

- Body Scan Meditation: Sit or lie down comfortably. Close your eyes and slowly scan your body from head to toe, noticing any tension or discomfort. Breathe into these areas, imagining the tension melting away with each exhale. Spend 10 minutes on this exercise, focusing on relaxation and release.

Tools for Tracking Emotional and Physical Progress

1. Emotional State:
   On a scale of 1 to 10, how would you rate your emotional state today? (1 = Very low, 10 = Very high)
   Your Rating: _____

2. Physical Energy:
   On a scale of 1 to 10, how would you rate your energy levels today? (1 = Very low, 10 = Very high)
   Your Rating: _____

3. Overall Well-Being:
   On a scale of 1 to 10, how would you rate your overall well-being today? (1 = Poor, 10 = Excellent)
   Your Rating: _____

Reflection

Write one or two sentences reflecting on why you gave the ratings above. Consider how the day's activities, emotions, or physical state influenced these ratings.

Example Reflection

"Today, reflecting on the physical impact of trauma reminded me of the tension I often feel in my shoulders. My emotional state felt a bit strained, so I rated it at a 5. The body scan meditation helped ease some of this tension, which brought my physical energy up to a 6. Overall, I would rate my well-being at a 6 because I feel more aware of the physical effects of my trauma and more equipped to address them."

Day 4
Recognizing Trauma Triggers

"Trauma triggers are like landmines—they can be hidden but are always there."
— Unknown

Focus

Today, we'll identify the triggers that bring your trauma to the surface. Recognizing these triggers is an important step in managing them and reducing their impact on your daily life.

Daily Prompt

Reflect on the situations, people, or places that trigger memories or feelings related to your trauma. How do these triggers affect you, and how do you usually respond when they arise?

Exercise

- Reflective Writing: Write about a specific trigger that consistently brings up your trauma. How does this trigger affect you, both emotionally and physically? How do you usually cope with it?

- Identifying and Managing Triggers: List three common triggers you've noticed. For each, describe how you typically respond and explore strategies you might use to manage or reduce the impact of these triggers.

_____

_____

_____

_____

_____

Visualization and Mindfulness

- Grounding Visualization: Close your eyes and imagine a safe, calm place where you feel completely at ease. This could be a real place or a creation of your imagination. Spend a few minutes visualizing yourself in this place whenever you feel triggered, focusing on the peace and safety it brings you.

Tools for Tracking Emotional and Physical Progress

1. Emotional State:
   On a scale of 1 to 10, how would you rate your emotional state today? (1 = Very low, 10 = Very high)
   Your Rating: _____

2. Physical Energy:
    On a scale of 1 to 10, how would you rate your energy levels
    today? (1 = Very low, 10 = Very high)
    Your Rating: _____

3. Overall Well-Being:
    On a scale of 1 to 10, how would you rate your overall
    well-being today? (1 = Poor, 10 = Excellent)
    Your Rating: _____

Reflection

Write one or two sentences reflecting on why you gave
the ratings above. Consider how the day's activities, emotions, or
physical state influenced these ratings.

Example Reflection

"Today, I identified a few triggers that consistently bring
up difficult memories, which left my emotional state feeling
a bit fragile, so I rated it at a 4. However, using the grounding
visualization gave me a sense of calm, raising my physical energy
to a 6. Overall, I would rate my well-being at a 5 because, while
the triggers were challenging, the exercise provided a helpful tool
for managing them."

Day 5
Resilience in the Face of Trauma

---

*"Do not judge me by my success, judge me by how
many times I fell down and got back up again."*
— Nelson Mandela

Focus

Today, we'll focus on the concept of resilience and how
you've demonstrated resilience in the face of trauma. Resilience
isn't just about surviving; it's about finding ways to thrive
despite challenges.

Daily Prompt

Reflect on a time when you demonstrated resilience. What
did you do to cope with the challenge, and what strengths did you
discover in yourself during this experience?

Exercise

- Reflective Writing: Write about a specific instance where
  you bounced back from a difficult situation. What personal

qualities helped you persevere? How did this experience shape your understanding of your own resilience?

- Resilience Inventory: List three personal strengths that have helped you navigate trauma. For each strength, write about a time when it served you well and how it contributed to your resilience.

_____

_____

_____

_____

_____

Visualization and Mindfulness

- Visualization of Strength: Close your eyes and visualize yourself overcoming a challenge. Imagine the strength and resilience you used in that moment and let that feeling fill your body with confidence and power. Spend a few minutes sitting with this sense of inner strength.

Tools for Tracking Emotional and Physical Progress

1. Emotional State:
   On a scale of 1 to 10, how would you rate your emotional state today? (1 = Very low, 10 = Very high)
   Your Rating: _____

2. Physical Energy:
   On a scale of 1 to 10, how would you rate your energy levels today? (1 = Very low, 10 = Very high)
   Your Rating: _____

3. Overall Well-Being:
   On a scale of 1 to 10, how would you rate your overall
   well-being today? (1 = Poor, 10 = Excellent)
   Your Rating: _____

Reflection

Write one or two sentences reflecting on why you gave
the ratings above. Consider how the day's activities, emotions, or
physical state influenced these ratings.

Example Reflection

"Today, reflecting on my resilience reminded me of how far
I've come. My emotional state felt strong, so I rated it at a 7. The
visualization exercise helped reinforce my sense of inner strength,
boosting my physical energy to a 7 as well. Overall, I would rate
my well-being at a 7 because I feel empowered by recognizing
my resilience."

Day 6
Reframing Trauma as a Path to Growth

---

*"The human capacity for burden is like bamboo—far
more flexible than you'd ever believe at first glance."*
— Jodi Picoult

Focus

Today, we'll explore the idea of post-traumatic growth—the
concept that, through facing and overcoming trauma, we can
develop new strengths, perspectives, and a deeper appreciation
for life.

Daily Prompt

Consider how your trauma has changed you—not just in
terms of the pain, but in terms of the growth it has prompted.
What positive changes have emerged from your challenges, and
how has your perspective on life shifted?

Exercise

- Reflective Writing: Write about a way in which you've grown as a result of your trauma. What new strengths, insights, or perspectives have you gained through your experiences?
- Growth Visualization: Imagine your life as a garden. Reflect on how the "seeds" of your trauma have grown into something new and strong. Write about what your garden looks like now, and what you hope it will become as you continue to heal.

_____

_____

_____

_____

_____

Visualization and Mindfulness

- Visualization of Growth: Close your eyes and visualize a seed growing into a strong tree. As the tree grows, imagine your own personal growth and strength expanding, despite the storms it has weathered. Spend a few minutes focusing on this image of growth and resilience.

Tools for Tracking Emotional and Physical Progress

1. Emotional State:
   On a scale of 1 to 10, how would you rate your emotional state today? (1 = Very low, 10 = Very high)
   Your Rating: _____

2. Physical Energy:
   On a scale of 1 to 10, how would you rate your energy levels today? (1 = Very low, 10 = Very high)
   Your Rating: _____

3. Overall Well-Being:
   On a scale of 1 to 10, how would you rate your overall well-being today? (1 = Poor, 10 = Excellent)
   Your Rating: _____

Reflection

Write one or two sentences reflecting on why you gave the ratings above. Consider how the day's activities, emotions, or physical state influenced these ratings.

Example Reflection

"Today, focusing on how I've grown through my trauma helped me see the positive changes I've experienced. My emotional state felt more optimistic, so I rated it at a 6. The growth visualization reinforced my sense of progress, raising my physical energy to a 7. Overall, I would rate my well-being at a 7 because I feel hopeful about the future."

Day 7
Reflection and Growth

"The journey of healing is not about becoming someone new, but about becoming more of who you really are."
— Unknown

Focus

Today marks the end of our second week. We'll reflect on the lessons learned about trauma and resilience and set intentions for the coming weeks.

Daily Prompt

Reflect on what you've learned this week about your trauma and resilience. How has your understanding of trauma deepened, and what insights have you gained about your own strength and capacity for growth?

Exercise

- Reflective Writing: Summarize the key insights you've gained this week. What stood out to you the most? How have these insights changed your perspective on your trauma and your healing journey?
- Setting Intentions: Write down three intentions for the next week. These might be areas of focus, attitudes you want to cultivate, or practices you want to continue as you deepen your understanding of trauma and resilience.

_____

_____

_____

_____

_____

Visualization and Mindfulness

- Mindful Breathing: Spend a few minutes in mindful breathing, focusing on the breath as it enters and leaves your body. With each exhale, let go of any tension or stress from the past week. With each inhale, invite in calm and focus for the week ahead.

Tools for Tracking Emotional and Physical Progress

1. Emotional State:
   On a scale of 1 to 10, how would you rate your emotional state today? (1 = Very low, 10 = Very high)
   Your Rating: _____

2. Physical Energy:
    On a scale of 1 to 10, how would you rate your energy levels
    today? (1 = Very low, 10 = Very high)
    Your Rating: _____

3. Overall Well-Being:
    On a scale of 1 to 10, how would you rate your overall
    well-being today? (1 = Poor, 10 = Excellent)
    Your Rating: _____

Reflection

Write one or two sentences reflecting on why you gave
the ratings above. Consider how the day's activities, emotions, or
physical state influenced these ratings.

Example Reflection

"Today, reflecting on the week as a whole made me feel
proud of the progress I've made. My emotional state felt balanced,
so I rated it at a 7. The mindful breathing exercise helped me
release some lingering stress, which brought my physical energy
to a 6. Overall, I would rate my well-being at a 7 because I feel
prepared and motivated for the week ahead."

Weekly Recap
Week 2
Recognizing and Understanding
Personal Trauma

Reflecting on Your Journey

Congratulations on completing Week 2! This week, you've made significant strides in recognizing and understanding the traumas that have shaped your life. You've explored the emotional and physical impacts of trauma, identified your triggers, and discovered how resilience has played a role in your journey.

Key Insights

1. Identifying Trauma:
   - You've taken the courageous step of identifying the specific traumas that have impacted your life. Acknowledging these events is the first step toward healing.

2. Understanding Emotional and Physical Impact:
   - This week, you've reflected on how trauma manifests both emotionally and physically. You've recognized the deep

connections between your experiences and your well-being, which is essential for holistic healing.

3. Recognizing Triggers and Building Resilience:
    *   By identifying the triggers that bring your trauma to the surface, you've begun to develop strategies to manage them. You've also explored how resilience has helped you navigate these challenges, reinforcing your inner strength.

Tracking Your Progress

Now, let's review your emotional and physical well-being over the past week. Consider your daily ratings and reflect on the patterns you've noticed:

Progress Reflection Prompt

*   What patterns have you observed in your emotional and physical well-being this week?
*   Were there specific days when you felt particularly impacted by your trauma?
*   What factors contributed to these feelings, and how did your resilience help you navigate them?
*   How did the exercises, mindfulness practices, and visualization techniques influence your well-being?

Your Reflection

_____

_____

_____

_____

_____

_____

Looking Ahead

As you move into the next week, think about the areas where you'd like to continue focusing your energy. What insights from this week will you carry forward? What intentions do you want to set for the upcoming days?

Setting Intentions

- Intention 1: _____
- Intention 2: _____
- Intention 3: _____

Remember, healing is a journey that requires patience and bravery. Take pride in the progress you've made this week and stay dedicated to your path of growth and resilience. You're doing remarkable work—continue moving forward with strength and purpose.

Week 3
Building Emotional Resilience

Day 1
Emotional Awareness

"Awareness is the greatest agent for change."
— Eckhart Tolle

Focus

Today, we'll begin by increasing our emotional awareness. Understanding and naming your emotions is the first step in managing them effectively and building resilience.

Daily Prompt

Reflect on how well you understand your own emotions. How often do you pause to recognize and name what you're feeling? What emotions have you noticed coming up most frequently?

Exercise

- Reflective Writing: Spend 10 minutes writing about the emotions you've experienced today. How did you feel, and how did you respond to those emotions?

- Emotional Awareness Practice: Throughout the day, whenever you notice an emotion, pause to name it and explore where it's coming from. Write down any insights that come up.

_____

_____

_____

_____

_____

Visualization and Mindfulness

- Mindful Emotion Scan: Close your eyes and take a few deep breaths. Slowly scan your body and mind, noticing any emotions present. Allow yourself to sit with each emotion without judgment, simply observing it as it is.

Tools for Tracking Emotional and Physical Progress

1. Emotional State:
   On a scale of 1 to 10, how would you rate your emotional state today? (1 = Very low, 10 = Very high)
   Your Rating: _____

2. Physical Energy:
   On a scale of 1 to 10, how would you rate your energy levels today? (1 = Very low, 10 = Very high)
   Your Rating: _____

3. Overall Well-Being:
   On a scale of 1 to 10, how would you rate your overall
   well-being today? (1 = Poor, 10 = Excellent)
   Your Rating: _____

Reflection

Write one or two sentences reflecting on why you gave
the ratings above. Consider how the day's activities, emotions, or
physical state influenced these ratings.

Example Reflection

"Today, I noticed a lot of frustration bubbling up, which
made me rate my emotional state at a 4. However, after naming
the emotion and sitting with it, I felt more in control, which
brought my overall well-being to a 6."

Day 2
Stress Management Techniques

"It's not the load that breaks you down,
it's the way you carry it."
— Lou Holtz

Focus

Today, we'll focus on developing effective stress management techniques. Learning how to manage stress is crucial for emotional resilience and overall well-being.

Daily Prompt

Reflect on how you currently manage stress. What techniques work for you, and which ones might need improvement? How does stress manifest in your body and mind?

Exercise

- Reflective Writing: Write about the ways stress shows up in your life and how you usually cope with it. Are there specific techniques that help you feel more balanced?

- Stress Management Practice: Experiment with a new stress management technique today, such as deep breathing, progressive muscle relaxation, or mindful walking. Reflect on how it affects your stress levels.

_____

_____

_____

_____

_____

Visualization and Mindfulness

- Breath Awareness: Practice deep, intentional breathing throughout the day. Inhale slowly for a count of 4, hold for 4, and exhale for 6. Focus on the calming effect of each breath.

Tools for Tracking Emotional and Physical Progress

1. Emotional State:
   On a scale of 1 to 10, how would you rate your emotional state today? (1 = Very low, 10 = Very high)
   Your Rating: _____

2. Physical Energy:
   On a scale of 1 to 10, how would you rate your energy levels today? (1 = Very low, 10 = Very high)
   Your Rating: _____

3. Overall Well-Being:
   On a scale of 1 to 10, how would you rate your overall
   well-being today? (1 = Poor, 10 = Excellent)
   Your Rating: _____

Reflection

Write one or two sentences reflecting on why you gave
the ratings above. Consider how the day's activities, emotions, or
physical state influenced these ratings.

Example Reflection

"Today, I felt a lot of tension in my shoulders due to
stress, so I rated my physical energy at a 5. After practicing deep
breathing, I felt the tension ease, which improved my emotional
state to a 6."

Day 3
Cultivating a Positive Mindset

"A positive mindset brings positive things."
— Unknown

Focus

Today, we'll work on cultivating a positive mindset. Your thoughts have a powerful influence on your emotions and resilience, so learning to foster positivity is key to emotional well-being.

Daily Prompt

Reflect on how you talk to yourself in difficult times. What role does self-talk play in your ability to stay positive? How might shifting your self-talk toward positivity change your emotional experience?

Exercise

- Reflective Writing: Write about the self-talk you've noticed today. How has it influenced your emotions? If you caught

yourself in negative self-talk, how did you shift it to
something more positive?

- Positive Self-Talk Practice: Practice positive self-talk
  throughout the day. Whenever you notice negative
  thoughts, consciously replace them with affirmations or
  positive statements. Write down any shifts in your mood or
  mindset.

_____

_____

_____

_____

_____

Visualization and Mindfulness

- Affirmation Meditation: Sit comfortably, close your eyes,
  and repeat a positive affirmation silently to yourself for a
  few minutes. Focus on the meaning of the words and how
  they make you feel.

Tools for Tracking Emotional and Physical Progress

1. Emotional State:
   On a scale of 1 to 10, how would you rate your emotional state
   today? (1 = Very low, 10 = Very high)
   Your Rating: _____

2. Physical Energy:
   On a scale of 1 to 10, how would you rate your energy levels
   today? (1 = Very low, 10 = Very high)
   Your Rating: _____

3. Overall Well-Being:
   On a scale of 1 to 10, how would you rate your overall
   well-being today? (1 = Poor, 10 = Excellent)
   Your Rating: _____

Reflection

Write one or two sentences reflecting on why you gave
the ratings above. Consider how the day's activities, emotions, or
physical state influenced these ratings.

Example Reflection

"Today, I caught myself in a negative thought spiral and
shifted to positive affirmations, which improved my emotional
state to a 7. My physical energy also felt better, at a 6, because I
was less weighed down by stress."

Day 4
Emotional Boundaries

*"You are not required to set yourself on fire
to keep others warm."*
— Unknown

Focus

Today, we'll focus on the importance of setting and maintaining emotional boundaries. Healthy boundaries are essential for protecting your emotional well-being and building resilience.

Daily Prompt

Reflect on your emotional boundaries. How well do you protect your emotional space? Are there areas in your life where your boundaries need strengthening?

Exercise

- Reflective Writing: Write about a situation where you've allowed your boundaries to be crossed. How did it make you feel, and how might you handle it differently in the future?

- Boundary Setting Practice: Identify a specific area where you need stronger emotional boundaries. Write down one action you can take today to reinforce this boundary.

_____

_____

_____

_____

_____

Visualization and Mindfulness

- Boundary Visualization: Close your eyes and imagine yourself surrounded by a protective bubble. This bubble allows in positive energy but keeps out negativity. Spend a few minutes visualizing this boundary and how it feels to be within it.

Tools for Tracking Emotional and Physical Progress

1. Emotional State:
   On a scale of 1 to 10, how would you rate your emotional state today? (1 = Very low, 10 = Very high)
   Your Rating: _____

2. Physical Energy:
   On a scale of 1 to 10, how would you rate your energy levels today? (1 = Very low, 10 = Very high)
   Your Rating: _____

3. Overall Well-Being:
   On a scale of 1 to 10, how would you rate your overall
   well-being today? (1 = Poor, 10 = Excellent)
   Your Rating: _____

Reflection

Write one or two sentences reflecting on why you gave
the ratings above. Consider how the day's activities, emotions, or
physical state influenced these ratings.

Example Reflection

"Today, setting emotional boundaries was challenging, and
my emotional state fluctuated between a 4 and a 6. However, the
boundary visualization exercise helped me feel more protected,
which raised my overall well-being to a 6."

Day 5
The Power of Gratitude

"Gratitude turns what we have into enough."
— Melody Beattie

Focus

Today, we'll explore the power of gratitude in enhancing emotional resilience. Cultivating gratitude helps shift your focus from what's lackingto what's abundant, fostering a more positive mindset.

Daily Prompt

Reflect on the role gratitude plays in your life. How can cultivating gratitude improve your emotional resilience and overall well-being?

Exercise

- Reflective Writing: Start a gratitude list today. Write down three things you're grateful for and reflect on how these positive aspects of your life contribute to your resilience.
- Gratitude Practice: Throughout the day, consciously notice and appreciate small moments of joy or beauty. Add these to your gratitude list as they occur.

_____
_____
_____
_____
_____

Visualization and Mindfulness

- Gratitude Visualization: Close your eyes and visualize each item on your gratitude list. Imagine them filling you with warmth and light, spreading a sense of contentment throughout your body.

Tools for Tracking Emotional and Physical Progress

1. Emotional State:
   On a scale of 1 to 10, how would you rate your emotional state today? (1 = Very low, 10 = Very high)
   Your Rating: _____

2. Physical Energy:
   On a scale of 1 to 10, how would you rate your energy levels today? (1 = Very low, 10 = Very high)
   Your Rating: _____

3. Overall Well-Being:
   On a scale of 1 to 10, how would you rate your overall well-being today? (1 = Poor, 10 = Excellent)
   Your Rating: _____

Reflection

Write one or two sentences reflecting on why you gave the ratings above. Consider how the day's activities, emotions, or physical state influenced these ratings.

Example Reflection

"Today, focusing on gratitude helped me shift my emotional state from a 5 to a 7. My physical energy felt more vibrant at a 7, thanks to the positive outlook I cultivated."

Day 6
Managing Emotional Overwhelm

"You don't have to control your thoughts.
You just have to stop letting them control you."
— Dan Millman

Focus

Today, we'll focus on strategies for managing emotional overwhelm. Learning how to navigate overwhelming emotions is crucial for maintaining emotional resilience.

Daily Prompt

Reflect on what situations or thoughts typically lead to emotional overwhelm. How do you usually cope when you feel overwhelmed, and what strategies might help you manage these feelings more effectively?

Exercise

- Reflective Writing: Write about a recent experience of emotional overwhelm. What triggered it, and how did you respond? What might you do differently next time to better manage your emotions?

- Overwhelm Management Plan: Develop a plan for managing emotional overwhelm. Include specific steps you can take when you feel emotions beginning to escalate, such as deep breathing, stepping away from the situation, or practicing mindfulness.

_____

_____

_____

_____

_____

Visualization and Mindfulness

- Calm Centering Exercise: Sit quietly and focus on your breath. With each inhale, imagine drawing in calm energy; with each exhale, imagine releasing stress. Continue this for a few minutes, allowing your body and mind to find their center.

Tools for Tracking Emotional and Physical Progress

1. Emotional State:
   On a scale of 1 to 10, how would you rate your emotional state today? (1 = Very low, 10 = Very high)
   Your Rating: _____

2. Physical Energy:
   On a scale of 1 to 10, how would you rate your energy levels today? (1 = Very low, 10 = Very high)
   Your Rating: _____

3. Overall Well-Being:
   On a scale of 1 to 10, how would you rate your overall well-being today? (1 = Poor, 10 = Excellent)
   Your Rating: _____

Reflection

Write one or two sentences reflecting on why you gave the ratings above. Consider how the day's activities, emotions, or physical state influenced these ratings.

Example Reflection

"Today, emotional overwhelm was challenging, so I rated my emotional state at a 4. However, after using my overwhelm management plan, I felt more centered, which brought my overall well-being to a 6."

Day 7
Reflection and Growth

*"Strength doesn't come from what you can do.
It comes from overcoming the things
you once thought you couldn't."*
— Rikki Rogers

Focus

Today, we'll reflect on the emotional resilience tools you've practiced throughout the week. This reflection will help you consolidate your learnings and set the stage for continued growth.

Daily Prompt

Reflect on the emotional resilience tools you've practiced this week. Which ones felt most effective, and how have they changed your emotional experience? How has your ability to manage stress, cultivate positivity, and set boundaries improved?

Exercise

- Reflective Writing: Summarize the key lessons and insights you've gained about emotional resilience this week. What strategies will you continue to practice? How has your emotional awareness and resilience evolved?
- Setting Intentions: Write down three intentions for the next week, focusing on how you can continue to build emotional resilience.

_____

_____

_____

_____

_____

Visualization and Mindfulness

- Mindful Reflection: Spend a few minutes in quiet reflection, focusing on the progress you've made this week. As you breathe in, imagine drawing in strength and resilience; as you breathe out, release any tension or self-doubt.

Tools for Tracking Emotional and Physical Progress

1. Emotional State:
   On a scale of 1 to 10, how would you rate your emotional state today? (1 = Very low, 10 = Very high)
   Your Rating: _____

2. Physical Energy:
   On a scale of 1 to 10, how would you rate your energy levels today? (1 = Very low, 10 = Very high)
   Your Rating: _____

3. Overall Well-Being:
   On a scale of 1 to 10, how would you rate your overall well-being today? (1 = Poor, 10 = Excellent)
   Your Rating: _____

Reflection

Write one or two sentences reflecting on why you gave the ratings above. Consider how the day's activities, emotions, or physical state influenced these ratings.

Example Reflection

"Today, reflecting on the week as a whole made me feel proud of the progress I've made. My emotional state felt balanced, so I rated it at a 7. The mindful breathing exercise helped center me, raising my physical energy to a 7 as well."

Weekly Recap
Week 3
Building Emotional Resilience

Reflecting on Your Journey

Congratulations on completing Week 3! This week, you've worked hard on building emotional resilience. You've explored your emotional awareness, stress management techniques, and the power of positive thinking, boundaries, and gratitude.

Key Insights

1. Emotional Awareness:
   - You've deepened your understanding of your emotions and how to identify and manage them. Recognizing and naming your emotions has helped you become more attuned to your emotional needs.

2. Stress Management:
   - This week, you've practiced various stress management techniques. Whether through deep breathing, mindfulness, or progressive relaxation, you've started to build a toolkit to help you cope with stress effectively.

3. Cultivating Positivity:
   • You've explored the power of positive thinking and how self-talk can influence your emotional state. Shifting towards positivity has allowed you to manage challenges with greater ease.

4. Setting Boundaries:
   • You've learned the importance of setting emotional boundaries to protect your well-being. Establishing and maintaining these boundaries has strengthened your resilience.

5. Gratitude:
   • Practicing gratitude has shifted your focus to the abundance in your life, enhancing your emotional resilience and overall well-being.

Tracking Your Progress

Now, let's take a moment to look back at your emotional and physical well-being over the past week. Review your daily ratings for emotional state, physical energy, and overall well-being. Consider the following prompt as you reflect on the patterns you've noticed:

Progress Reflection Prompt

What patterns have you observed in your emotional and physical well-being this week?
- Were there specific days when you felt particularly strong or vulnerable?
- What factors contributed to these fluctuations?

- How did the exercises and mindfulness practices influence your well-being?

Your Reflection

_____

_____

_____

_____

_____

_____

Looking Ahead

As you prepare for the next week, think about the areas where you'd like to focus your energy. What lessons from this week will you carry forward? What intentions do you want to set for the upcoming days?

Setting Intentions

- Intention 1: _____
- Intention 2: _____
- Intention 3: _____

Remember, this journey is about progress, not perfection. Celebrate the steps you've taken this week and look forward to the growth that lies ahead. You're doing incredible work—keep moving forward with strength and resilience.

Week 4
Cultivating Growth
and Strength

Day 1
Recognizing Emotional Growth

"The only journey is the one within."
— Rainer Maria Rilke

Focus

Today, we'll start by recognizing the emotional growth you've experienced throughout this journey. Growth often happens slowly, so it's important to take time to reflect on the changes within yourself.

Daily Prompt

Think about where you were emotionally when you began this journal. How have your emotions evolved? What growth have you noticed in your ability to manage difficult feelings or situations?

Exercise

- Reflective Writing: Spend 10 minutes writing about the emotional growth you've experienced. Consider specific moments or challenges where you responded differently than you might have in the past.

- Growth Recognition Practice: Throughout the day, whenever you notice an emotion, take a moment to acknowledge how your response has changed over time. Write down any instances where you notice this growth.

_____

_____

_____

_____

_____

Visualization and Mindfulness

- Emotional Growth Visualization: Close your eyes and visualize a plant growing from a seed into a strong, healthy tree. Imagine this plant represents your emotional growth— nurtured by the challenges and experiences you've faced.

Tools for Tracking Emotional and Physical Progress

1. Emotional State:
   On a scale of 1 to 10, how would you rate your emotional state today? (1 = Very low, 10 = Very high)
   Your Rating: _____

2. Physical Energy:
   On a scale of 1 to 10, how would you rate your energy levels today? (1 = Very low, 10 = Very high)
   Your Rating: _____

3. Overall Well-Being:
   On a scale of 1 to 10, how would you rate your overall
   well-being today? (1 = Poor, 10 = Excellent)
   Your Rating: _____

Reflection

Write one or two sentences reflecting on why you gave
the ratings above. Consider how the day's activities, emotions, or
physical state influenced these ratings.

Example Reflection

"Today, I noticed that I was more patient with myself when
a difficult emotion arose, which I rated as a 7 for emotional state.
My physical energy remained steady at a 6, and overall, I felt like I
was growing, so I rated my well-being at a 7."

Day 2
Building on Physical Strength

"Take care of your body.
It's the only place you have to live."
— Jim Rohn

Focus

Today, we'll focus on the importance of physical strength as a foundation for resilience. Taking care of your body through exercise, nutrition, and rest is crucial for overall well-being.

Daily Prompt

Reflect on your physical health and how it impacts your emotional well-being. What physical activities make you feel strong and energized? How has your physical strength changed during this journey?

Exercise

- Reflective Writing: Write about how you've been taking care of your physical health. Are there areas where you've seen improvement? Where might you want to focus more attention?

- Physical Strength Practice: Engage in a physical activity today that makes you feel strong—whether it's a walk, yoga, or a workout. Reflect on how this activity influences your emotional state.

_____

_____

_____

_____

_____

Visualization and Mindfulness

- Body Awareness Meditation: Spend a few minutes in quiet reflection, focusing on different parts of your body. Notice how they feel and any areas of tension or strength. Breathe deeply into these areas, inviting in relaxation and strength.

Tools for Tracking Emotional and Physical Progress

1. Emotional State:
   On a scale of 1 to 10, how would you rate your emotional state today? (1 = Very low, 10 = Very high)
   Your Rating: _____

2. Physical Energy:
   On a scale of 1 to 10, how would you rate your energy levels today? (1 = Very low, 10 = Very high)
   Your Rating: _____

3. Overall Well-Being:
   On a scale of 1 to 10, how would you rate your overall well-being today? (1 = Poor, 10 = Excellent)
   Your Rating: _____

Reflection

Write one or two sentences reflecting on why you gave the ratings above. Consider how the day's activities, emotions, or physical state influenced these ratings.

Example Reflection

"After a brisk walk today, I felt my physical energy increase to an 8. This also boosted my emotional state to a 7, as I felt more grounded and centered. My overall well-being felt strong at an 8, thanks to taking care of my body."

Day 3
Nurturing Personal Strengths

---

*"What lies behind us and what lies before us
are tiny matters compared to what lies within us."*
— Ralph Waldo Emerson

Focus

Today, we'll focus on nurturing the personal strengths that have emerged through your healing journey. Recognizing and cultivating these strengths is key to continued growth.

Daily Prompt

Reflect on the personal strengths you've discovered during this journey. What qualities or skills have emerged that you didn't recognize before? How can you continue to nurture these strengths?

Exercise

• Reflective Writing: Write about a strength that has become more apparent to you over the past weeks. How has this strength supported you in your healing journey? What can you do to continue nurturing this strength?

- Strength-Building Practice: Identify a situation today where you can consciously apply this strength. Reflect on how it felt to use this strength in a real-world context.

_____

_____

_____

_____

_____

Visualization and Mindfulness

- Inner Strength Visualization: Close your eyes and visualize a glowing light within you that represents your inner strength. Imagine this light growing brighter and stronger with each breath, filling you with confidence and resilience.

Tools for Tracking Emotional and Physical Progress

1. Emotional State:
   On a scale of 1 to 10, how would you rate your emotional state today? (1 = Very low, 10 = Very high)
   Your Rating: _____

2. Physical Energy:
   On a scale of 1 to 10, how would you rate your energy levels today? (1 = Very low, 10 = Very high)
   Your Rating: _____

3. Overall Well-Being:
   On a scale of 1 to 10, how would you rate your overall
   well-being today? (1 = Poor, 10 = Excellent)
   Your Rating: _____

Reflection

Write one or two sentences reflecting on why you gave
the ratings above. Consider how the day's activities, emotions, or
physical state influenced these ratings.

Example Reflection

"Today, I focused on using my newfound patience in a
stressful situation, which helped keep my emotional state at a 7.
My physical energy remained steady at a 6, but I felt more capable
and resilient, so my overall well-being rated at an 8."

Day 4
Establishing Healthy Habits

"We are what we repeatedly do.
Excellence, then, is not an act, but a habit."
— Aristotle

Focus

Today, we'll focus on creating and maintaining healthy habits that support both your emotional and physical well-being. Healthy habits are the foundation of long-term growth and resilience.

Daily Prompt

Reflect on the habits you've developed or want to develop during this journey. Which habits have supported your growth? What new habits would you like to establish to further your progress?

Exercise

- Reflective Writing: Write about a habit that has been particularly supportive of your emotional or physical well-being. What has made this habit effective? What steps can you take to ensure this habit remains a part of your routine?
- Habit Formation Practice: Choose one new healthy habit to focus on today. Practice this habit with intention and reflect on how it influences your overall well-being.

_____

_____

_____

_____

_____

Visualization and Mindfulness

- Healthy Habit Visualization: Close your eyes and imagine yourself successfully incorporating a new healthy habit into your daily life. Visualize the positive impact this habit has on your emotional and physical health.

Tools for Tracking Emotional and Physical Progress

1. Emotional State:
   On a scale of 1 to 10, how would you rate your emotional state today? (1 = Very low, 10 = Very high)
   Your Rating: _____

2. Physical Energy:
   On a scale of 1 to 10, how would you rate your energy levels today? (1 = Very low, 10 = Very high)
   Your Rating: _____

3. Overall Well-Being:
   On a scale of 1 to 10, how would you rate your overall well-being today? (1 = Poor, 10 = Excellent)
   Your Rating: _____

Reflection

Write one or two sentences reflecting on why you gave the ratings above. Consider how the day's activities, emotions, or physical state influenced these ratings.

Example Reflection

"Today, I focused on establishing a new habit of drinking more water, which helped boost my physical energy to a 7. My emotional state also improved, as I felt more hydrated and clear-headed, rating it at a 7. Overall, I would rate my well-being at a 7 because I felt good about the new habit."

Day 5
Integrating Emotional and Physical Growth

"To keep the body in good health is a duty...
otherwise we shall not be able to keep our
mind strong and clear."
— Buddha

Focus

Today, we'll explore how emotional and physical growth work together to support your overall resilience. Understanding this connection can help you maintain balance and well-being in all areas of life.

Daily Prompt

Reflect on how your emotional and physical growth have influenced each other. How has your physical well-being supported your emotional growth, and vice versa? How can you continue to integrate these aspects of your life?

Exercise

- Reflective Writing: Write about a time when improving your physical health positively influenced your emotional state, or when emotional growth led to better physical well-being. How do these two aspects of growth support each other?
- Integration Practice: Choose an activity today that supports both your emotional and physical well-being, such as a walk in nature, yoga, or a mindfulness practice. Reflect on how this activity enhances both aspects of your growth.

_____

_____

_____

_____

_____

Visualization and Mindfulness

- Integration Visualization: Close your eyes and visualize a strong, balanced structure representing your emotional and physical growth. Imagine these two aspects of yourself working together in harmony, supporting and strengthening each other.

Tools for Tracking Emotional and Physical Progress

1. Emotional State:
   On a scale of 1 to 10, how would you rate your emotional state today? (1 = Very low, 10 = Very high)
   Your Rating: _____

2. Physical Energy:
   On a scale of 1 to 10, how would you rate your energy levels
   today? (1 = Very low, 10 = Very high)
   Your Rating: _____

3. Overall Well-Being:
   On a scale of 1 to 10, how would you rate your overall
   well-being today? (1 = Poor, 10 = Excellent)
   Your Rating: _____

Reflection

Write one or two sentences reflecting on why you gave
the ratings above. Consider how the day's activities, emotions, or
physical state influenced these ratings.

Example Reflection

"Today, practicing yoga helped me feel more centered
emotionally, raising my emotional state to an 8. My physical
energy was a bit lower at a 6, but overall, the integration of both
aspects made me feel balanced, so I rated my well-being at a 7."

Day 6
Overcoming Challenges in Growth

"Difficulties strengthen the mind,
as labor does the body."
— Seneca

Focus

Today, we'll focus on recognizing and overcoming challenges or setbacks in the growth process. Challenges are a natural part of growth, and learning how to navigate them is key to building resilience.

Daily Prompt

Reflect on any challenges or setbacks you've encountered in your growth journey. How have you responded to these challenges? What strategies have helped you overcome obstacles, and how can you apply them in the future?

Exercise

- Reflective Writing: Write about a challenge you've faced during this journey and how you overcame it. What did you learn from this experience? How has it strengthened your resilience?
- Challenge Management Practice: Identify a current challenge you're facing. Develop a plan for addressing this challenge using the strategies you've learned. Reflect on how this approach influences your emotional and physical well-being.

_____

_____

_____

_____

_____

Visualization and Mindfulness

- Overcoming Challenges Visualization: Close your eyes and visualize a mountain representing your current challenge. Imagine yourself climbing the mountain, overcoming obstacles with strength and determination, and reaching the summit.

Tools for Tracking Emotional and Physical Progress

1. Emotional State:
   On a scale of 1 to 10, how would you rate your emotional state today? (1 = Very low, 10 = Very high)
   Your Rating: _____

2. Physical Energy:
   On a scale of 1 to 10, how would you rate your energy levels today? (1 = Very low, 10 = Very high)
   Your Rating: _____

3. Overall Well-Being:
   On a scale of 1 to 10, how would you rate your overall well-being today? (1 = Poor, 10 = Excellent)
   Your Rating: _____

Reflection

Write one or two sentences reflecting on why you gave the ratings above. Consider how the day's activities, emotions, or physical state influenced these ratings.

Example Reflection

"Today, facing a challenging situation made me feel emotionally drained, rating my emotional state at a 5. However, after reflecting on past challenges and planning how to address this one, I felt more confident, which brought my overall well-being to a 6."

Day 7
Reflection and Setting Intentions
for Continued Growth

---

*"Strength doesn't come from what you can do.
It comes from overcoming the things
you once thought you couldn't."*
— Rikki Rogers

Focus

Today, we'll reflect on the growth and strength you've cultivated throughout the week. This reflection will help you consolidate your learnings and set the stage for continued growth.

Daily Prompt

Reflect on the growth and strength you've cultivated this week. How have you seen yourself change, and what new strengths have emerged? How can you continue to build on this foundation in the coming weeks?

Exercise

- Reflective Writing: Summarize the key lessons and insights you've gained about growth and strength this week. What strategies will you continue to practice? How has your resilience evolved?
- Setting Intentions: Write down three intentions for the next week, focusing on how you can continue to build growth and strength.

_____

_____

_____

_____

_____

Visualization and Mindfulness

- Mindful Reflection: Spend a few minutes in quiet reflection, focusing on the progress you've made this week. As you breathe in, imagine drawing in strength and resilience; as you breathe out, release any tension or self-doubt.

Tools for Tracking Emotional and Physical Progress

1. Emotional State:
   On a scale of 1 to 10, how would you rate your emotional state today? (1 = Very low, 10 = Very high)
   Your Rating: _____

2. Physical Energy:
   On a scale of 1 to 10, how would you rate your energy levels today? (1 = Very low, 10 = Very high)
   Your Rating: _____

3. Overall Well-Being:
   On a scale of 1 to 10, how would you rate your overall well-being today? (1 = Poor, 10 = Excellent)
   Your Rating: _____

Reflection

Write one or two sentences reflecting on why you gave the ratings above. Consider how the day's activities, emotions, or physical state influenced these ratings.

Example Reflection

"Today, reflecting on my growth this week made me feel proud of my progress, rating my emotional state at an 8. My physical energy felt balanced at a 7, and overall, I rated my well-being at an 8 because I feel strong and ready for the week ahead."

Weekly Recap
Week 4
Cultivating Growth and Strength

Reflecting on Your Journey

Congratulations on completing Week 4! This week, you've focused on cultivating both emotional and physical growth and strength. You've recognized your progress, nurtured your personal strengths, and established healthy habits that support your overall well-being. Let's take a moment to reflect on the key insights you've gained and set intentions for continued growth.

Key Insights

1. Recognizing Emotional Growth:
   - You've taken the time to reflect on your emotional journey and acknowledged the growth you've experienced. Recognizing this progress is vital in building confidence and self-awareness.

2. Building Physical Strength:
   - This week, you've explored the connection between physical health and emotional resilience. You've focused on how maintaining your physical well-being supports your emotional state and overall resilience.

3. Nurturing Personal Strengths:
   - You've identified and nurtured personal strengths that have emerged through your healing journey. These strengths are a testament to your resilience and will continue to support you in overcoming challenges.

4. Establishing Healthy Habits:
   - You've started to build and reinforce healthy habits that contribute to your emotional and physical well-being. These habits are the foundation for long-term growth and resilience.

5. Overcoming Challenges:
   - This week, you've also recognized and addressed challenges in your growth journey. By applying the strategies you've learned, you've strengthened your resilience and developed a deeper understanding of your capacity to overcome obstacles.

Tracking Your Progress

Now, let's review your emotional and physical well-being over the past week. Consider your daily ratings and reflect on the patterns you've noticed:

Progress Reflection Prompt

- What patterns have you observed in your emotional and physical well-being this week?
- Were there specific days when you felt particularly strong or challenged?
- What factors contributed to these feelings, and how did your strengths and resilience help you navigate them?
- How did the exercises, mindfulness practices, and visualization techniques influence your well-being?

Your Reflection

_____

_____

_____

_____

_____

Looking Ahead

As you prepare for the next week, think about the areas where you'd like to continue focusing your energy. What insights from this week will you carry forward? What intentions do you want to set for the upcoming days?

Setting Intentions

- Intention 1: _____
- Intention 2: _____
- Intention 3: _____

Remember, growth and strength are cultivated over time, through consistent effort and reflection. Celebrate the progress you've made this week and stay committed to your path of resilience and well-being. You're doing remarkable work—continue to nurture your growth and move forward with strength and confidence.

Post-Assessment

Understanding Trauma and Building Resilience

The Post-Assessment is designed to help you reflect on your progress over the past 30 days. This is a moment to celebrate your courage, honesty, and dedication to your healing journey. By revisiting the initial self-assessment, you can see in a tangible way just how much you've grown in your understanding of trauma, your ability to build resilience, and your overall emotional and physical well-being.

Over the past month, you've confronted difficult truths, explored deep emotions, and embraced the process of healing with an open heart. Now is the time to take stock of all that effort. This assessment is not just a reflection of where you are today, but a testament to the strength and resilience you've developed along the way.

As you work through this Post-Assessment, allow yourself to acknowledge your achievements—no matter how big or small. Celebrate the progress you've made and take pride in the steps you've taken to become more resilient, more self-aware, and more in tune with your own needs. At the same time, consider the areas where you want to continue growing. This isn't the end of your journey; it's a checkpoint that shows you just how far you've come and guides you toward where you want to go next.

Remember, this is your opportunity to recognize the powerful, positive changes you've made in your life. Embrace this moment with the same courage and honesty that you've shown throughout this journey. You've done incredible work, and now it's time to see that growth reflected back to you in a meaningful way.

Post-Assessment Structured Reflection

Section 1 Knowledge and Understanding

Reflect on Your Understanding of Trauma

1. How has your understanding of trauma changed after completing this journal?
   - Reflect on how your definition of trauma has evolved. Have you gained new insights into the different types of trauma and how they impact individuals differently?

   Your Response:

   _____

   _____

   _____

2. Can you now identify different types of trauma more clearly?
   ☐ Yes
   ☐ No

   Reflect: What new types of trauma have you become aware of?
   Your Response:

   _____

   _____

   _____

Section 2 Coping Mechanisms

Reflect on Your Coping Mechanisms

1. Have you learned any new coping mechanisms over the past 30 days?
   ☐ Yes
   ☐ No

   Reflect: Which new coping strategies have you found most effective?
   Your Response:

   _____
   _____
   _____

2. How has your ability to cope with trauma improved?
   • On a scale of 1 to 10, rate how confident you feel in your ability to manage the effects of trauma now compared to the start of this journal.
   • Your Rating: _____

Section 3 Emotional and Physical Responses

Reflect on Your Emotional State

1. How has your emotional state changed since you began this journey?
   - Compare your emotional responses now to how you felt at the start of the journal. What shifts have you noticed in your emotional regulation?

   Your Response:

   _____

   _____

   _____

2. What changes have you noticed in your physical responses to trauma?
   - On a scale of 1 to 10, rate the effectiveness of guided visualizations and mindfulness activities in managing your physical responses.
   - Your Rating: _____

   Reflect: How have these practices influenced your overall well-being?
   Your Response:

   _____

   _____

   _____

Section 4 Personal Growth

Reflect on Your Personal Growth

1. Do you feel more resilient after completing this journal?
   ☐ Yes
   ☐ No

   Reflect: In what ways have you become more resilient?
   Your Response:

   _____
   _____
   _____

2. How do you plan to continue building resilience in your daily life?
   • Outline any strategies or practices you intend to keep using to maintain and further develop your resilience.

   Your Response:

   _____
   _____
   _____

As you conclude this part of your journey, I want to take a moment to acknowledge the courage, dedication, and resilience you've shown throughout this process. Healing is not a linear path, and the work you've done here is significant. You've taken important steps toward understanding your trauma and building the resilience to move forward with strength.

But remember, healing is ongoing. I invite you to continue exploring your inner world and nurturing your growth. Whether it's through more journaling, reading, or seeking further support, know that you are not alone on this journey. I'm here, and there are many resources available to support your continued progress.

Thank you for allowing me to be a part of your healing process. I look forward to continuing this work together.

With deep respect and unwavering belief in your strength,

Dr. Lisa M. Wineburg

About the Author

Dr. Lisa M. Wineburg is a renowned therapist and trauma specialist with over 20 years of experience in the field. She has dedicated her career to helping individuals overcome trauma and build resilience. Her work is grounded in both research and personal experience, which she shares in her best-selling book, *Beyond the Scars*. Dr. Wineburg is also a sought-after speaker and a compassionate advocate for mental health awareness. Through her writings and teachings, she aims to empower people to transform their pain into strength and to live fulfilling, resilient lives.

Note About
Beyond the Scars: Navigating Personal Growth After Trauma
By Lisa M Wineburg

Unlock your journey of healing and empowerment with Dr. Lisa M. Wineburg's "Beyond the Scars: Navigating Personal Growth After Trauma."

In this powerful guide, Dr. Wineburg, a trauma survivor and mental health professional, blends her personal story with transformative psychological insights. This book serves as a beacon for anyone looking to move from surviving to thriving after trauma.

Inside "Beyond the Scars," you'll find:

- Personal Narratives: Dr. Wineburg's own journey offers a relatable path to overcoming adversity.
- Healing Strategies: Trauma-informed exercises and resilience-building techniques to support your recovery.
- Emotional Wellness Tools: Learn to harness post-traumatic growth and reshape your life's narrative.
- Expert Insights: Psychological perspectives that underpin the trauma recovery process.

Start Your Transformation

"*Beyond the Scars*" is a must-read for trauma survivors, mental health professionals, and anyone ready to turn pain into power. Take the first step towards reclaiming your life.

- ISBN-13: 978-1-957506-97-5 (paperback)
- ISBN-13: 978-1-957506-99-9 (hardback)

Available on Amazon.

If You Enjoyed This Journal, Please Leave a Review

Your feedback is incredibly valuable. If this journal has helped you in any way, I would be grateful if you could take a moment to leave a review. Sharing your thoughts not only helps me continue creating resources that support healing and growth, but it also guides others who may be on a similar journey. Your words could inspire someone else to take the first step towards their own healing.

Thank you for your support and for being a part of this journey.

www.ingramcontent.com/pod-product-compliance
Lightning Source LLC
Chambersburg PA
CBHW031515120626
46545CB00005B/1892